Math
Connections

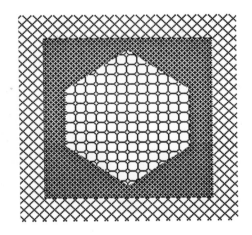

David J. Glatzer
Joyce Glatzer

DALE SEYMOUR PUBLICATIONS

Editor: Patty Holubar
Cover design: Rachel Gage

Order number DS01901
ISBN 0-86651-463-5

DALE
SEYMOUR
PUBLICATIONS
P.O. BOX 10888
PALO ALTO, CA 94303

8 9 10 -ML- 99 98 97 96

Contents

Introduction

Purpose

The purpose of these blackline masters is to provide classroom math teachers with a variety of nonroutine problem activities that will foster the development of critical thinking skills and will reinforce concepts from the math curriculum. The activities are intended for grades 7–9. However, each activity may be adapted to other grade levels.

Philosophy

Asking questions is the chief means used by classroom teachers to monitor and assess student learning. The authors of this program believe that simple recall and comprehension questions are not enough to help students reach higher levels of learning. Critical thinking skills need to be nurtured by constant practice in the math classroom. Textbooks do not always provide students such practice. In addition, it is essential for students to have opportunities to express math understanding through written expression. Again, standard textbooks do not provide such opportunities.

Background on Bloom

Benjamin Bloom has developed a classification of educational outcomes and questions that range from the simple to the complex. To move the students to higher levels of thinking, you should ask questions on the higher levels of Bloom's taxonomy. The levels are as follows:

1. Knowledge—ability to recall information
2. Comprehension—ability to understand, translate, and interpret information
3. Application—ability to apply information
4. Analysis—ability to break material into its parts
5. Synthesis—ability to create new situations, to put parts together
6. Evaluation—ability to judge information according to established criteria

As you use the activities in this book, you will see that your students are functioning on the higher levels of the taxonomy.

Organization

The book is organized in six sections, each with a different activity format. Each section contains problems from several content categories, such as fractions, decimals, percents, number theory, geometry, measurement, and pre-algebra. The problems are arranged in order of difficulty.

Suggested answers are provided in the Answer Section of this book, although for many problems the students may come up with other acceptable solutions or rationales. As a model, the first problem on each page is answered for the student.

Each page in a section concludes with a follow-up problem called Completing the Connection. The problem is meant to help you assess the students' overall understanding of the activity and to help the students attain closure. Students will benefit from working on these problems in small groups. Finally, each section contains an introduction that discusses the section's activity, works through sample problems, and describes the section's follow-up problems.

Use of the Material

There is no one way to use this book. It can be adapted to the needs of your students. However, they will receive the greatest benefit if you provide opportunities for them to share the thought processes they used in arriving at their answers.

- Classroom discussion—Make a photocopy of the page for each student and a transparency of the same page for yourself. Discuss the problems one at a time, encouraging the students to support their answers.

- Small-group work—Divide the students into small groups (of, say, four each), and have each group complete

the page. Each group then shares its work with the rest of the class.

- Share with a neighbor—Ask the students to complete the page independently and then share their responses with a partner.

- Student-generated extensions— When the class finishes a page, ask the students to write additional problems of the same form. (For an example of this, see the Completing the Connection problems for Section 2.)

Conclusion

Remember that the activities in this book:

- Can be used at any time of the year
- Can be used to provide variety in the math curriculum
- Can be used for preview and review
- Can be used to increase student involvement
- Are easily adaptable
- Are open-ended and easily extended
- Are fun

The ideas contained in this book have been used successfully in classrooms at the middle and secondary levels.

Math Connections

Section 1

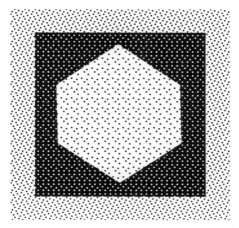

Versus

Introduction

The Versus activity deals with key math ideas in which the critical attribute is the contrast between two concepts. In math, contrasting concepts are often studied at the same time. Because of this, the students need practice in differentiating between contrasting ideas.

Before the students begin the exercise on a page, it would be beneficial for you to review the definitions of the contrasting concepts presented. For example, if you were introducing the sample exercise on the following page, it would be appropriate to review the definitions of odd numbers and even numbers, stressing that even numbers are divisible by 2 and end in the digit 0, 2, 4, 6, or 8.

SAMPLE EXERCISE

Write an X to show whether each number is
odd, even, neither, or can't be determined.

	Item	Odd	Even	Neither	Can't Be Determined
1.	16		X		
2.	10,001	X			
3.	$\frac{1}{2}$			X	
4.	3x				X

To complete each problem in this section, the students are expected to
place items in one of four categories. The first two categories represent
the contrasting concepts; the third, the possibility that the item fits neither
concept; and the final, the possibility that the classification cannot be
determined from the information given. In the sample exercise above, the
students are expected to check each number against the definitions for
odd and even numbers in order to determine which category to mark. The
answers for the exercise indicate that 16 can be determined to be even,
that 10,001 is odd, but $\frac{1}{2}$ by definition is neither. In the case of 3x, the
students need to remember that a variable can represent any number and
hence the classification cannot be determined.

Some exercises in this section allow the students to demonstrate their
understanding of the contrasting concepts by completing reversal
problems, in which one of the contrasting items is provided, along with the
classification. The students must provide the other contrasting item. For
example, problem 7 in "Complement versus Supplement" provides 62° for
the first angle and complementary for the classification. To satisfy that
classification, the students must write 28° for the second angle.

To assess the students' understanding of this activity, a follow-up
question on each page has been included. In it the students are asked to
identify the key characteristic they used to classify the items on that page.
Encourage the students to be as specific as possible. For example, when
dealing with odd and even numbers, they might respond that the key
characteristic they used was divisibility by 2. Another activity in this
section contrasts positive and negative numbers. There the characteristic
might be the comparison of the number to 0. Besides serving as an
assessment tool, these Completing the Connection questions provide the
students an opportunity to summarize the concepts learned in the activity
and help them attain closure.

MATH CONNECTIONS

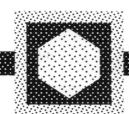

Positive vs. Negative

Write an X to show whether each item is positive,
negative, neither, or can't be determined.

	Item	Positive	Negative	Neither	Can't Be Determined
1.	6	X			
2.	−2.1				
3.	$\frac{3}{7}$				
4.	$-1\frac{1}{3}$				
5.	0				
6.	$|-14|$				
7.	$(-1)^4$				
8.	$3a$				
9.	gain of 6 yards in football				
10.	change in temperature from 3°C to1°C				

COMPLETING THE CONNECTION
What was the major characteristic you used to determine
whether the item was positive or negative?

Greater Than vs. Less Than

Write an X to show whether the first item in each row is less than the second item, greater than the second item, neither, or can't be determined. When the X is provided, supply the missing item. (Answers may vary.)

	First Item	Second Item	1st < 2nd	1st > 2nd	Neither	Can't Be Determined
1.	17	16.9		X		
2.	$\frac{3}{7}$	$\frac{3}{8}$				
3.	$\frac{7}{10}$	$\frac{70}{100}$				
4.	$\frac{1}{3}$	0.33				
5.	acute <	obtuse <				
6.	$\sqrt{25}$	$\sqrt{16} + \sqrt{9}$				
7.	$\frac{1}{2}$% of 80	50% of 80				
8.	a^2	a^3				
9.	0.0001			X		
10.		$-2\frac{1}{3}$	X			

COMPLETING THE CONNECTION

What was the major characteristic you used to determine whether the first item was greater than or less than the second item?

Factor vs. Multiple

Write an X to show whether the first number in each row is a factor of the second number, a multiple of the second number, neither, or can't be determined. When the X is provided, supply the missing number. (Answers may vary.)

	First Number	Second Number	1st is Factor of 2nd	1st is Multiple of 2nd	Neither	Can't Be Determined
1.	3	6	X			
2.	14	7				
3.	1,000	1,000,000				
4.	50	125				
5.	(4)(3)(2)	(3)(2)				
6.	2^5	2^4				
7.	6a	12b				
8.	12xy	12y				
9.	1		X			
10.	0			X		

COMPLETING THE CONNECTION

What was the major characteristic you used to determine whether the first number was a factor or a multiple of the second number?

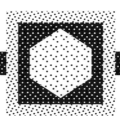

Prime vs. Composite

Write an X to show whether each number is prime,
composite, neither, or can't be determined.

	Number	Prime	Composite	Neither	Can't Be Determined
1.	2	X			
2.	12				
3.	51				
4.	1				
5.	999				
6.	1341				
7.	1001				
8.	x				
9.	3^4				
10.	$\sqrt{289}$				

COMPLETING THE CONNECTION

What was the major characteristic you used to determine
whether the number was prime or composite?

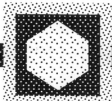

Complement vs. Supplement

Write an X to show whether the two angles in each row are
complementary, supplementary, neither, or can't be determined.
When the X is provided, supply the missing angle.

	First Angle	Second Angle	Comple- mentary	Supple- mentary	Neither	Can't Be Determined
1.	45°	45°	X			
2.	90°	90°				
3.	80°	80°				
4.	50°	50°				
5.	111°	69°				
6.	1°	89°				
7.	62°		X			
8.		100°		X		
9.	$k°$		X			
10.	$r°$			X		

COMPLETING THE CONNECTION

What was the major characteristic you used to determine whether the two
angles were complementary or supplementary?

Square vs. Square Root

Write an X to show whether the first number in each row is the square of the second number, the square root of the second number, neither, or can't be determined. When the X is provided, supply the missing number.

	First Number	Second Number	1st is Square of 2nd	1st is Square Root of 2nd	Neither	Can't Be Determined
1.	5	25		X		
2.	81	9				
3.	7	14				
4.	$\frac{1}{2}$	$\frac{1}{4}$				
5.	0.1	0.2				
6.	1.4	0.2				
7.	3^2	3^4				
8.	a^2	b^2				
9.	144		X			
10.	0.2			X		

COMPLETING THE CONNECTION

What was the major characteristic you used to determine whether the first number was the square or the square root of the second number?

MATH CONNECTIONS

Parallel vs. Perpendicular

Write an X to show whether the first line in each row is parallel to the second line, perpendicular to the second line, neither, or can't be determined. When the X is provided, supply the missing line. (Answers may vary.)

	First Line	Second Line	1st || 2nd	1st ⊥ 2nd	Neither	Can't Be Determined
1.	$y = 3x$	$y = 3x + 7$	X			
2.	$y = 2x + 1$	$y = -2x + 1$				
3.	$y = 2x$	$y = -\frac{1}{2}x + 8$				
4.	$y = 3$	$y = -3$				
5.	$y = 1$	$x = 1$				
6.	$y = x$	$y = -x$				
7.	$y = 4x$	$y = kx$				
8.	$y = 6x - 3$		X			
9.	$y = -\frac{1}{4}x$			X		
10.	$y = x$				X	

COMPLETING THE CONNECTION

What was the major characteristic you used to determine whether the lines for the equations given were parallel or perpendicular?

Section 2

Which One Doesn't Belong?

Introduction

The Which One Doesn't Belong? activity allows the students to concentrate on the critical attributes associated with specific topics in math. They are asked to determine how three of four given items are related. Recognition of relationships and patterns is fundamental for success in math. Furthermore, the ability to verbalize these relationships is necessary to ensure understanding. In stating the rationale for a response, the students must indicate the characteristic common to the three related items.

SAMPLE EXERCISE

In each row, circle the item that does not belong. Be prepared to give the reason for your answer. Answers may vary.

	A	B	C	D
1.	50%	$\frac{1}{2}$	0.5	$\boxed{\frac{1}{5}}$ not equivalent to 50%
2.	② not odd number	3	5	⑨ not prime number

In each problem in this section, the students are asked to examine the four items and select the oddball, the item that doesn't belong with the other three. For example, in problem 1 in the sample exercise, a possible answer is D, since the other three items are equivalent to 50%. However, since the directions are open-ended, it is possible that different students will come up with different answers for any given problem. For example, in problem 2 in the sample exercise, one possible answer is A, since the other three are odd numbers. Another possible answer is D, since the other three are prime numbers.

Note that in giving A as an answer for problem 2, the students may want to respond that 2 is an even number. Although this is so, in giving their rationale, the students should always respond with the property common to the three related items.

To assess the students' understanding of this activity, the follow-up problem on each page asks the students to create their own Which One Doesn't Belong? problem for a category provided. Although all the students are dealing with the same conditions, they will write different problems. It would thus be beneficial for them to share their ideas in a class discussion. For instance, in the Completing the Connection problem for "Fractions and Decimals," the students are asked to list four fractions, three of which are between $\frac{1}{2}$ and 1 and one of which is not. Many sets of answers are possible—for example,

$$\frac{2}{3}, \frac{3}{4}, \frac{3}{5}, \frac{3}{2}$$

$$\frac{7}{8}, \frac{8}{9}, \frac{9}{10}, \frac{2}{7}$$

$$\frac{4}{9}, \frac{4}{5}, \frac{7}{10}, \frac{9}{11}$$

MATH CONNECTIONS

Fractions and Decimals

In each row, circle the item that does not belong. Be prepared to give the reason for your answer. Answers may vary.

	A	B	C	D
1.	$3\frac{1}{2}$	$\frac{7}{2}$	3.5	⑦.2 not equivalent to 3.5
2.	$\frac{21}{28}$	$\frac{15}{20}$	$\frac{30}{40}$	$\frac{15}{60}$
3.	$\frac{1}{5}, \frac{4}{5}$	$\frac{4}{9}, \frac{4}{9}$	$\frac{2}{3}, \frac{1}{3}$	$\frac{3}{8}, \frac{5}{8}$
4.	$\frac{18}{24}$	$\frac{25}{36}$	$\frac{51}{68}$	$\frac{26}{39}$
5.	$\frac{7}{3}$	$\frac{8}{5}$	$\frac{11}{6}$	$\frac{23}{12}$
6.	0.125	0.875	0.555	0.375
7.	0.08	$\frac{4}{5}$	0.8	$\frac{12}{15}$
8.	$\frac{1}{2}$ of $\frac{1}{4}$	$\frac{1}{5}$ of $\frac{5}{8}$	$\frac{1}{2}$ of 16	$\frac{1}{16}$ of 2

COMPLETING THE CONNECTION

List four fractions such that three of the fractions are between $\frac{1}{2}$ and 1 and one of the fractions is not between $\frac{1}{2}$ and 1.

Percents

In each row, circle the item that does not belong. Be prepared to give the reason for your answer. Answers may vary.

	A	B	C	D
1.	$\frac{3}{4}$	0.75	not equivalent to 75% (0.34)	75%
2.	20% of 40	40% of 20	10% of 80	5% of 20
3.	1 cent	1%	1 centimeter	1° F
4.	$3\frac{1}{4}$	0.325	3.25	325%
5.	50% of 18	18 (0.5)	$\frac{1}{2}$ % of 18	18% of 50
6.	$100 at 6% for 2 years	$100 at 8% for 1 year	$100 at 2% for 4 years	$100 at 4% for 2 years
7.	percent change from 80 to 120	percent change from 66 to 99	percent change from 40 to 80	percent change from 48 to 72
8.	percent change from 100 to 90	percent change from 50 to 45	percent change from 200 to 180	percent change from 60 to 50

COMPLETING THE CONNECTION

List four ratios such that three of the ratios are equivalent to 10% and one of the ratios is not equivalent to 10%.

MATH CONNECTIONS

Number Theory

In each row, circle the item that does not belong. Be prepared to give the reason for your answer. Answers may vary.

	A	B	C	D
1.	21	not divisible by 7 (67)	77	63
2.	31	51	11	17
3.	1000	144	225	36
4.	72	27	342	343
5.	4	9	12	24
6.	36	128	8	32
7.	1	8	27	100
8.	3.4×10^3	2.5×10^{-2}	65×10^3	1.1×10^5

COMPLETING THE CONNECTION

List four numbers such that three of the numbers are multiples of 11 and one of the numbers is not a multiple of 11.

Measurement

In each row, circle the item that does not belong. Be prepared to give the reason for your answer. Answers may vary.

	A	B	C	D
1.	3 feet	36 inches	1 yard	(1 meter) not equivalent to 1 yard
2.	ounce	pound	gram	yard
3.	pint	gallon	liter	quart
4.	milli-	centi-	kilo-	pro-
5.	10 years	1 decade	$\frac{1}{10}$ century	365 days
6.	$\frac{1}{4}$ inch	$\frac{1}{5}$ inch	$\frac{1}{16}$ inch	$\frac{1}{8}$ inch
7.	100	6 dozen	$\frac{1}{2}$ gross	72
8.	1 square yard	144 square inches	1296 square inches	9 square feet

COMPLETING THE CONNECTION

List four measurements such that three of them are measurements of length and one of them is not a measurement of length.

MATH CONNECTIONS

Geometry

In each row, circle the item that does not belong. Be prepared to give the reason for your answer. Answers may vary.

	A	B	C	D
1.	20°	37°	83°	(94°) *not acute*
2.	30° and 60°	70° and 20°	44° and 46°	55° and 45°
3.	130° and 60°	45° and 135°	110° and 70°	90° and 90°
4.	10°, 30°, 140°	30°, 60°, 90°	50°, 60°, 80°	55°, 65°, 60°
5.	equilateral	scalene	isosceles	acute
6.	acute	right	scalene	obtuse
7.	pentagon	rhombus	trapezoid	rectangle
8.	3, 4, 5	6, 7, 8	5, 12, 13	8, 15, 17

COMPLETING THE CONNECTION

List the names of four polygons such that three of the names
are for polygons of five or more sides and one of the names
is not for a polygon of five or more sides.

Geometry Visual

In each row, circle the item that does not belong. Be prepared to give the reason for your answer. Answers may vary.

	A	B	C	D
1.	triangle	triangle	*not an acute triangle* (circled shape)	triangle
2.	parallelogram 5, 5, 5, 5	square 4, 4, 4, 4	parallelogram 5, 5, 5, 5	rectangle 7, 4, 4, 7
3.	pentagon	concave polygon	hexagon	triangle
4.	triangle	triangle	triangle	triangle
5.	lines/angles	lines/angles	lines/angles	lines/angles

COMPLETING THE CONNECTION

Draw four polygons such that three of the polygons are regular and one of the polygons is not regular.

MATH CONNECTIONS

Pre-Algebra

In each row, circle the item that does not belong. Be prepared to give the reason for your answer. Answers may vary.

	A	B	C	D
1.	$(-2)(-3)(-7)(4)$ product is not positive	$(-7)(-5)$	$-(-4)(5)$	$(-2)(-3)(5)$
2.	$3(x + 4) = 3x + 7$	$2(x + 5) = 2x + 10$	$5(x + 1) = 5x + 5$	$7(x + 4) = 7x + 28$
3.	$5x$	$4x$	$3y$	$-2x$
4.	$-(-49)$	$|-49|$	$(-7)^2$	-7^2
5.	$3a^2 b^2$	x^3	abc	$2^2 y^3$
6.	$\sqrt{18}$	$\sqrt{32}$	$\sqrt{48}$	$\sqrt{50}$
7.	$x^2 - 1$	$x^2 - b^2$	$9a^2 - 25b^2$	$x^2 + 1$
8.	$y = 2x + 1$	$2x - y = 4$	$6x - 3y = 9$	$2y = x + 7$

COMPLETING THE CONNECTION

List four sums such that three of the sums have a value of –5 and one of the sums does not have a value of –5.

Section 3

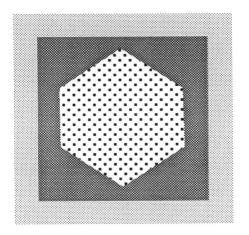

How Do You Know That?

Introduction

The How Do You Know That? activity provides an opportunity for the students to use words to express key concepts in math. The ability to explain relationships is a better indicator of comprehension than the mechanical completion of standard computational examples. Therefore, the focus of this activity is relationships rather than computation. Cooperative learning and divergent thinking are encouraged. In addition, this activity challenges the students to demonstrate number sense.

For each question presented in this section, the students are asked to write one or more complete sentences. Student responses will vary. In formulating responses, the students should use their knowledge of definitions and relationships and their estimation skills. A sample exercise follows.

SAMPLE EXERCISE

Write one or more complete sentences to answer each question.
Answers may vary.

1. How do you know that $\frac{4}{9}$ of 80 is less than 40?

   Because 4/9 is less than 1/2 and 40 is 1/2 of 80, 4/9 of 80 must be less than 40.

   or

   Since 1/9 of 80 is less than 9, 4/9 of 80 must be less than 36.

2. How do you know that 3 angles of a triangle can't measure 50°, 60°, and 80°?

   The sum of the angles of a triangle must be 180°, and the given angles sum to more than 180°.

To summarize this activity, the Completing the Connection problem asks the students to reflect on the concepts they used to answer the questions on each page. Specifically, they are asked to identify one concept for each page. For example, for "Fractions," the students might respond with the concept of "dividing a non-zero number by itself" for question 4 or the concept of "the common denominator in addition" for question 8. There is no one correct response for any of the summary questions; any concept the students use can be considered valid.

MATH CONNECTIONS

Fractions

Write one or more complete sentences to answer each question. Answers may vary.

1. How do you know that $\frac{3}{7}$ and $\frac{6}{12}$ are not equal ratios?

    3/7 is less than 1/2, and 6/12 is equal to 1/2.

2. How do you know that $\frac{1}{4}$ is greater than $\frac{1}{5}$?

3. How do you know that $5\frac{1}{4} \times 5$ does not equal $25\frac{1}{4}$?

4. How do you know that $\frac{1}{4} \div \frac{1}{4} = 1$?

5. How do you know that $8 \div \frac{1}{2} > 8$?

6. How do you know that $2\frac{1}{2} + 3\frac{2}{3} > 6$?

7. How do you know that a number times its reciprocal equals 1?

8. How do you know that $\frac{1}{2} + \frac{1}{3} \neq \frac{2}{5}$?

COMPLETING THE CONNECTION

Identify one concept that you used to answer a question on this page.

Decimals

Write one or more complete sentences to answer each question. Answers may vary.

1. How do you know that 12 × $1.95 is between $23 and $24?

    $1.95 is slightly less than $2.00, and $2.00 times 12 would be $24. Therefore, the product must be slightly less than $24.

2. How do you know that 16 × 3.12 is greater than 48 and less than 64?

3. How do you know that 2.04 × 1000 is greater than 2000?

4. How do you know that 0.7 + 0.5 > 1?

5. How do you know that 20 ÷ 0.5 > 20?

6. How do you know that 60 × 4.2 is the same as 6 × 42?

7. How do you know that 0.3 ≠ 1/3?

8. How do you know that 42×10^3 is not in scientific notation?

COMPLETING THE CONNECTION
Identify one concept that you used to answer a question on this page.

MATH CONNECTIONS

Percents

Write one or more complete sentences to answer each question. Answers may vary.

1. How do you know that 50% of *A* is not equal to $\frac{1}{2}$% of *A*?

   ½% of A is less than 1%, or 1/100, of A, while
   50% is equal to ½ of A.

2. How do you know that 16% of 45 = 45% of 16?

3. How do you know that 5% is not always the same as $5.00?

4. How do you know that 110% of 20 is greater than 20?

5. How do you know that $10\frac{1}{2}$% of 100 is between 10 and 11?

6. How do you know that doubling a price is the same as increasing the price 100%?

7. How do you know that 6% of $420 is greater than 12% of $200?

8. How do you know that 30 + 15 is the same as 150% of 30?

COMPLETING THE CONNECTION
Identify one concept that you used to answer a question on this page.

Number Theory

Write one or more complete sentences to answer each question. Answers may vary.

1. How do you know that 4 is not the greatest common factor of 8 and 24?

    If you divide 4 into 8 and 24, the quotients still contain a common factor. Therefore, 4 can't be the greatest common factor.

2. How do you know that 1000 is not divisible by 3?

3. How do you know that 4 is not the least common multiple for 4 and 8?

4. How do you know that if 3 numbers have an average of 15, their sum is 45?

5. How do you know that 9 is not a factor of 100?

6. How do you know that 200 is not a perfect square?

7. If *b* is a factor of 12, how do you know that *b* will also be a factor of 36?

8. If a number has an odd number of factors, how do you know that the number is a perfect square?

COMPLETING THE CONNECTION

Identify one concept that you used to answer a question on this page.

© Dale Seymour Publications   MATH CONNECTIONS

Geometry and Measurement

Write one or more complete sentences to answer each question. Answers may vary.

1. How do you know that a triangle can't have 2 obtuse angles?

   The sum of the 3 angles of a triangle must be 180°. If 2 angles were obtuse, the sum would be greater than 180°.

2. How do you know that there are not 12 square inches in 1 square foot?

3. How do you know that the ratio of 5 feet to 5 yards is not 1:1?

4. How do you know that a quart of milk should not cost more than 2 pints of milk?

5. How do you know that the area of a square is not doubled when each side is doubled?

6. How do you know that $\frac{1}{2}$ of an obtuse angle can't be an obtuse angle?

7. How do you know that a triangle can't have sides that are 6, 8, and 14 units long?

8. How do you know that 2 sides of a triangle can't be parallel?

COMPLETING THE CONNECTION

Identify one concept that you used to answer a question on this page.

Pre-Algebra

Write one or more complete sentences to answer each question. Answers may vary.

1. How do you know that (2, 5) is not the same point as (5, 2)?

    The point (2,5) is located 2 units to the right and 5 units up from (0,0). The point (5,2) is located 5 units to the right and 2 units up from (0,0).

2. How do you know that $4^5 = 2^{10}$?

3. How do you know that 9 is not a solution to the equation $24 = 4x + 12$?

4. How do you know that the product of 5 negative numbers is a negative number?

5. How do you know that $(5 + 4)^2 \neq 5^2 + 4^2$?

6. How do you know that $-5^2 \neq 25$?

7. How do you know that $\sqrt{39}$ is between 6 and 7?

8. How do you know that a^2 is not always the same as $2a$?

COMPLETING THE CONNECTION
Identify one concept that you used to answer a question on this page.

Section 4

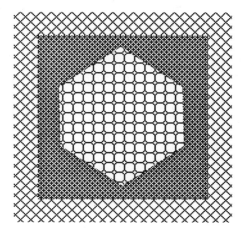

Write a Question Pictured

Introduction

The Write a Question Pictured activity reinforces math concepts and offers experience in using written expression. This activity provides the students with the opportunity to draw upon familiar relationships as they analyze data presented in a visual format.

SAMPLE EXERCISE

Using one or more complete sentences, write a word problem suggested
by each question mark. Answers may vary. (You do not have to give
the answer to the problem.)

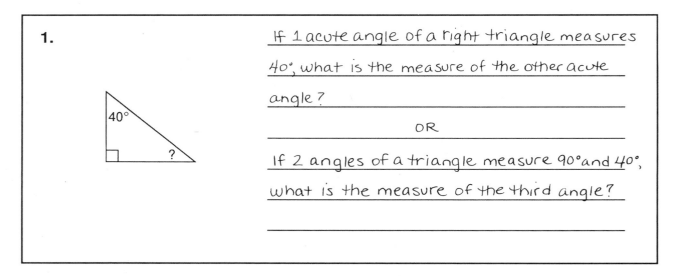

1.

If 1 acute angle of a right triangle measures
40°, what is the measure of the other acute
angle?

OR

If 2 angles of a triangle measure 90° and 40°,
what is the measure of the third angle?

To complete each problem in this section, the students analyze a
picture (or a calculation) and given information in order to determine the
implied question. Using one or more complete sentences, the students
write a word problem suggested by the question mark appearing in the
diagram (or calculation). Although only one word problem is required,
there may be different ways of expressing it. The students need not
provide a solution for the word problem they write.

For example, in analyzing the diagram in the sample exercise, the
students should consider information they know about angle relationships
in a triangle or, better yet, in a right triangle. On the basis of that analysis,
the students might offer either of the word problems shown. Both word
problems, however, get at the same question—the size of the angle noted
by the question mark in the diagram.

To help the students attain closure for this activity, the Completing the
Connection problem asks them to list two relationships presented on each
page. These relationships should be specific ones depicted in the
exercise. For instance, for "Triangles" the students could name the
Pythagorean theorem, the fact that equiangular triangles are also
equilateral, the concept of a median of a triangle, or the relationship
between sides in two similar triangles.

As a result of completing this section, the students see how important
a diagram is to the solution of a problem.

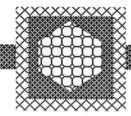

Geometry

Using one or more complete sentences, write a word problem suggested by each question mark. Answers may vary. (You do not have to give the answer to the problem.)

1. If 2 angles of a triangle measure 30° and 70°, what is the measure of the third angle?

2.

3.

4.

5.

COMPLETING THE CONNECTION
List two math relationships presented on this page.

MATH CONNECTIONS   © Dale Seymour Publications   33

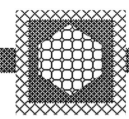

Geometry

Using one or more complete sentences, write a word problem suggested by each question mark. Answers may vary. (You do not have to give the answer to the problem.)

1.

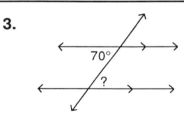

130°   110°
?
60°

If 3 angles of a quadrilateral measure 130°, 110°, and 60°, what is the measure of the fourth angle?

2.

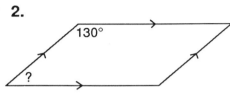

130°
?

_____
_____
_____

3.

70°
?

_____
_____
_____

4.

35° **?**

_____
_____
_____

5.

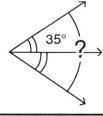

50°
? O
45°

_____
_____
_____

COMPLETING THE CONNECTION
List two math relationships presented on this page.

MATH CONNECTIONS

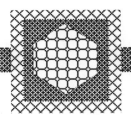

Triangles

Using one or more complete sentences, write a word problem suggested by each question mark. Answers may vary. (You do not have to give the answer to the problem.)

1.	15 ? 8	If the legs of a right triangle are 8 and 15 units, what is the length of the hypotenuse?
2.	? 7 ?	_____ _____ _____
3.	Median ? 10	_____ _____ _____
4.	5 ? Area = 30 square units	_____ _____ _____
5.	△ ABC ∿ △ DEF B 3 5 A 4 C E 9 ? D 12 F	_____ _____ _____

COMPLETING THE CONNECTION
List two math relationships presented on this page.

Quadrilaterals

Using one or more complete sentences, write a word problem suggested by each question mark. Answers may vary. (You do not have to give the answer to the problem.)

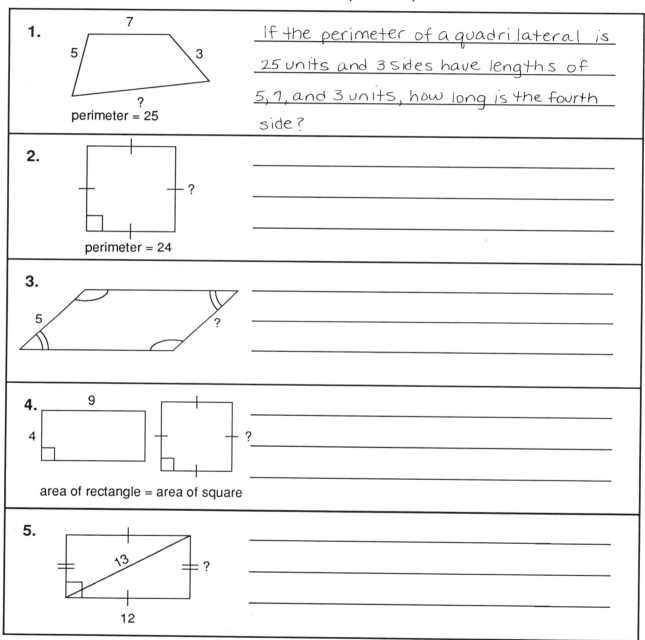

1.

7
5   3
?
perimeter = 25

If the perimeter of a quadrilateral is 25 units and 3 sides have lengths of 5, 7, and 3 units, how long is the fourth side?

2.

?
perimeter = 24

_____
_____
_____

3.

5
?

_____
_____
_____

4.

9
4
?
area of rectangle = area of square

_____
_____
_____

5.

13
12
?

_____
_____
_____

COMPLETING THE CONNECTION
List two math relationships presented on this page.

MATH CONNECTIONS

Circles

Using one or more complete sentences, write a word problem suggested by each question mark. Answers may vary. (You do not have to give the answer to the problem.)

1.		If the radius of a circle has a length of 5 units, what is the length of the diameter?
2.		
3.		
4.		
5.		

COMPLETING THE CONNECTION
List two math relationships presented on this page.

Coordinates

Using one or more complete sentences, write a word problem suggested by each question mark. Answers may vary. (You do not have to give the answer to the problem.)

1.

y axis, points (?, ?), (2, 4), (10, 4) on segment, *x* axis

If the endpoints of a line segment are (2, 4) and (10, 4), what are the coordinates of the midpoint?

2.

y axis with (2, 6) and (2, -8), ? label, *x* axis

3.

Square with vertices (4, 10), (?, ?), (4, 4), (12, 4)

4.

(-2, 2), 20, (?, 2)

5.

(1, 5), (5, 5), (?, ?)

COMPLETING THE CONNECTION
List two math relationships presented on this page.

Miscellaneous

Using one or more complete sentences, write a word problem suggested by each question mark. Answers may vary. (You do not have to give the answer to the problem.)

1.

$$\frac{50 + 60 + 70 + 80}{4} = ?$$

What is the average of the 4 numbers 50, 60, 70, and 80?

2.

$$\frac{50 + 60 + 70 + 80 + ?}{5} = 70$$

3.

$$5 + 2 \times \boxed{?} = 17$$

4.

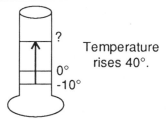

?

0°

-10°

Temperature rises 40°.

5.

A   B

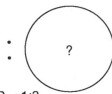

A:B = 1:3

COMPLETING THE CONNECTION

List two math relationships presented on this page.

Section 5

Help Me Pose
a Problem

Introduction

The Help Me Pose a Problem activity requires the students to identify
and provide the missing information that will allow a standard problem to
be solved. The underlying assumption to this activity is that as the
students are able to identify missing information, they will increase their
ability to solve and discuss a variety of standard problems.

SAMPLE EXERCISE

Write a complete sentence to provide the additional information needed to solve each problem. Answers may vary. (You do not have to give the answer to the problem.)

1. A rectangle has a perimeter of 24 feet. Find the area.

The rectangle has 1 dimension of 3 feet.

OR

The length of the rectangle is twice the width.

For each problem in this section, the students write a complete sentence to provide the additional information needed in order for the resulting problem to have a unique solution. For example, in the problem shown in the sample exercise, the students should be able to visualize several rectangles with a perimeter of 24 feet and note that these rectangles seem to have different areas:

To pin down a unique solution, the students must provide additional information that specifies which rectangle the problem refers to. The first answer given—that one dimension is 3 feet—is one possibility. This *new* information, along with the given perimeter, forces the rectangle to be 9 feet by 3 feet, with a resulting area of 27 square feet. The second answer—that the length is twice the width—is another possibility. This new piece of information, along with the given perimeter, forces the rectangle to be 8 feet by 4 feet, with a resulting area of 32 square feet.

When appropriate, encourage the students to use a diagram to help identify the missing information. You may also find it particularly beneficial in this activity to have the class discuss each problem and arrive at a consensus on the information to be added to the original statement of the problem.

In the answer key for this section, general rather than specific answers are given. These answers are meant as a guide for you; the students will give many specific answers in this open-ended activity.

To conclude each page, the students are asked in Completing the Connection to select any problem and explain why they feel the information they provided was necessary to complete the problem. This explanation should focus on the relationships among the concepts presented in the problem. For example, for the sample problem above, the students might respond, "Because the perimeter is given, providing 1 dimension of the rectangle established the second dimension. The 2 dimensions of the rectangle ultimately determine the area." Facility with such explanations is important if the students are to make progress in problem solving.

Ratios, Proportions, and Percents

Write a complete sentence to provide the additional information needed to solve each problem. Answers may vary. (You do not have to give the answer to the problem.)

1. The price of a T-shirt increased 10%. What was the new price?

   The original price of the T-shirt was $6.00.

2. Mrs. Levi purchased a television and paid $27.00 in sales tax. What was the rate of tax?

3. A store was offering a discount on sunglasses listed at $12.00. What was the sale price of the sunglasses?

4. In an orchard containing pear and apple trees, 42% of the trees are apple trees. How many apple trees are in the orchard?

5. Christopher can type a paper at the rate of 45 words per minute. How long will it take him to type his English term paper?

6. While playing basketball, Alicia made 8 free throws in 14 attempts. Nicole attempted free throws 20 times. Who was more successful?

COMPLETING THE CONNECTION

Select any problem on this page and explain why you feel the information you provided was necessary to complete the problem.

Number Theory

Write a complete sentence to provide the additional information needed to solve each problem. Answers may vary. (You do not have to give the answer to the problem.)

1. The average of 4 scores is 22. Find the largest score.

   The 3 smallest scores are 16, 19, and 25.

2. I am thinking of 3 consecutive odd numbers. What are the numbers?

3. I am thinking of a multiple of 5 between 70 and 100. What number is it?

4. I am thinking of a number that is a factor of both 16 and 72. What is the number?

5. Mr. Inaba wants to cut 3 strands of rope into as many pieces of equal length as he can. If the pieces are to be as long as possible and no rope is wasted, how long should each piece be?

6. The decorations committee plans to buy the same number of carnations and roses. Carnations come in bunches of 24, while roses come in smaller bunches. What is the least number of each flower the committee can buy?

COMPLETING THE CONNECTION

Select any problem on this page and explain why you feel the information you provided was necessary to complete the problem.

MATH CONNECTIONS

Pre-Algebra

Write a complete sentence to provide the additional information needed to solve each problem. Answers may vary. (You do not have to give the answer to the problem.)

1. The temperature at 6:00 A.M. was −5°F. During the day it rose. What temperature was reached at 2:00 P.M.?

   The temperature rose 3° each hour.

2. In the first 3 days of a 5-day cold spell, the lowest daily temperatures were −8°C, −5°C, and −1°C. What was the average temperature for the 5 days?

3. The product of 2 integers is −42. Find the integers.

4. The x-coordinate of point P is 7. In what quadrant is point P located?

5. A line segment has 1 endpoint at (3, 1). What are the coordinates of the midpoint of the line segment?

6. On the line 4 units above the x-axis are 2 points. The first point is (1, 4). Find the distance between the 2 points.

COMPLETING THE CONNECTION

Select any problem on this page and explain why you feel the information you provided was necessary to complete the problem.

Geometry

Write a complete sentence to provide the additional information needed to solve each problem. Answers may vary. (You do not have to give the answer to the problem.)

1. We have 2 angles that are supplementary. Find the measure of the larger angle.

   The measure of 1 angle is twice the measure of the other.

2. We have 2 unequal angles that are complementary. What is the measure of the smaller angle?

3. The first angle of a triangle is twice as large as the second. Find the measure of each angle of the triangle.

4. A quadrilateral has 2 right angles. Its other 2 angles are not right angles. Find the measure of the larger of these other 2 angles.

5. A right triangle has 1 leg with a length of 4 inches. Find the length of the hypotenuse.

6. A triangle has sides of 4, 6, and 7 inches. A second triangle is larger than the first triangle and has the same shape. How long is the longest side of the second triangle?

COMPLETING THE CONNECTION

Select any problem on this page and explain why you feel the information you provided was necessary to complete the problem.

MATH CONNECTIONS

Area, Perimeter, and Volume

Write a complete sentence to provide the additional information needed to solve each problem. Answers may vary. (You do not have to give the answer to the problem.)

1. The area of a rectangle is 18 square centimeters. Find the perimeter of the rectangle.

   The length of the rectangle is 9 centimeters.

2. The base of a triangle is 28 centimeters. Find the area of the triangle.

3. The perimeter of a square is equal to the perimeter of a rectangle with a length of 8 inches. Find the measure of the side of the square.

4. A rectangular solid has a volume of 60 cubic inches. What is the height of the rectangular solid?

5. Erica's mother wants to carpet a rectangular floor 26 feet long. How many square yards of carpet does she need?

6. Jabari drew a picture of 2 concentric circles. The smaller one had a radius of 4 inches. What is the area of the region between the 2 circles?

COMPLETING THE CONNECTION

Select any problem on this page and explain why you feel the information you provided was necessary to complete the problem.

Miscellaneous

Write a complete sentence to provide the additional information needed to solve each problem. Answers may vary. (You do not have to give the answer to the problem.)

1. Sam bought 1 notebook and 5 pencils for a total cost of $1.70. How much did the notebook cost him?

   The cost of each pencil was $0.12.

2. Hilke bought 3 record albums. The albums cost $7.98 each. How much change did she receive?

3. Juan has 9 individual pencils and 2 packages of pencils. How many pencils does Juan have in all?

4. A box of steel balls weighs 98 pounds. How much does each ball weigh?

5. A house costs 7 times more than the lot it stands on. What is the cost of the lot?

6. Lauren has more dimes than nickels. How many dimes does she have if the total amount of money she has is $4.20 and she has only nickels and dimes?

COMPLETING THE CONNECTION
Select any problem on this page and explain why you feel the information you provided was necessary to complete the problem.

             MATH CONNECTIONS

Section 6

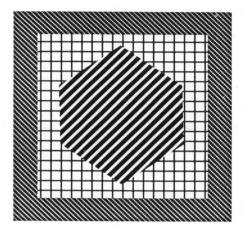

Quantitative Comparison

Introduction

The Quantitative Comparison activity, in yet another format, allows the students to demonstrate understanding of math concepts. They are to decide whether one quantity is greater than the other, whether the two quantities are equal, or whether the comparison cannot be made by using the given information. The objective of the activity is not complicated computation but comparison, which can frequently be accomplished by inspection. Thinking and estimation skills are essential for success in the activity.

SAMPLE EXERCISE

In each row, write A if the first item is greater, B if the second item is greater,
C if they are equal, and D if there's not enough information to decide.

	Given	First Item	Second Item	Response
1.		6^{12}	6^{13}	B
2.	$a > 1, b > 1$	a^{12}	b^{12}	D
3.		x^3	$(x^2)(x^1)$	C

To solve each quantitative comparison problem in this section, the students compare two quantities. If the first item is greater than the second, the students answer A. If the second item is greater than the first, the students answer B. If the two items are equal, the students answer C. If not enough information is given to make the comparison, the students answer D. For example, in comparing the two quantities in problem 1 in the sample exercise, the students should see that a product formed by thirteen 6's is greater than a product formed by twelve 6's. In comparing the items in problem 2, the students should realize that because there is no indication of the relationship between a and b, they cannot determine the response. This may lead them to feel that any problem involving variables will always have a response of D. Problem 3 is a counterexample to that premise: by definition, the two quantities in that problem are the same, regardless of the value assigned to x.

Quantitative comparison problems are versatile. They can be used for review, homework, warm-up, closure, or quizzes and tests. It should also be noted that quantitative comparison problems are a type that the students will see on certain college admission tests. When you use the problem as a classroom activity, it may prove helpful to have the students work in pairs so that they can monitor each other's tendency to do too much computation.

In the Completing the Connection follow-up for this section, the students are to explain the reasoning process they employed in making the comparison for any problem on each page. The explanation should be based on conceptual reasoning rather than on actual computation. For example, the explanation for problem 4 of "Geometry Visual" might be that the value of t must be less than 7 because the sum of the lengths of two sides of a triangle must be greater than the length of the third side. Other responses are also possible for this particular problem. Through evaluation of the explanations given by the students, you can help refine their reasoning processes.

MATH CONNECTIONS

Fractions

In each row, write A if the first item is greater, B if the second item is greater, C if they are equal, and D if there's not enough information to decide.

	First Item	Second Item	Response
1.	$2\frac{1}{2} + 2\frac{1}{2} + 2\frac{1}{2}$	$2\frac{1}{4} + 2\frac{1}{4} + 2\frac{1}{4}$	A
2.	$\frac{4}{9}$ of 82	50% of 82	
3.	$\frac{4}{11} + \frac{4}{11} + \frac{4}{11}$	1	
4.	$\frac{17}{51}$	$\frac{1}{3}$	
5.	$\frac{1}{a}$	$\frac{1}{b}$	
6.	$\frac{1}{2}$ of $\frac{1}{2}$ of $\frac{1}{2}$	$\frac{1}{6}$	
7.	the reciprocal of the reciprocal of $\frac{1}{7}$	$\frac{1}{7}$	
8.	$\frac{1}{10}$ of $\frac{1}{10}$	$\frac{1}{9}$ of $\frac{1}{11}$	

COMPLETING THE CONNECTION
Select any problem on this page and explain your thinking in arriving at the response you selected.

Decimals

In each row, write A if the first item is greater, B if the second item is greater, C if they are equal, and D if there's not enough information to decide.

	First Item	Second Item	Response
1.	$\frac{1}{2}$ of 18.5	4.5×2	A
2.	0.333	$\frac{1}{3}$	
3.	$0.4 + 0.3 + 0.7$	0.14	
4.	7.2×1000	720×100	
5.	$(0.9)^3$	$(0.9)^2$	
6.	2.06×10^4	20.6×10^3	
7.	$1 \div 0.1$	$0.1 \div 1$	
8.	$1.5(a)$	$a + 0.5a$	

COMPLETING THE CONNECTION

Select any problem on this page and explain your thinking in arriving at the response you selected.

MATH CONNECTIONS

Percents

In each row, write A if the first item is greater, B if the second item is greater,
C if they are equal, and D if there's not enough information to decide.

	First Item	Second Item	Response
1.	33% of 184	$\frac{1}{3}$ of 184	B
2.	the cost of an $80 radio at $10 off	the cost of an $80 radio at 10% off	
3.	$12\frac{1}{2}$% of 48	5	
4.	10% of a + 10% of a	20% of a	
5.	250% of 6	6 + 6 + 3	
6.	50% of 240	$\frac{1}{2}$% of 240	
7.	$100 increased 10%	$110 decreased 10%	
8.	a% of b	b% of a	

COMPLETING THE CONNECTION

Select any problem on this page and explain your thinking in
arriving at the response you selected.

Number Theory

In each row, write A if the first item is greater, B if the second item is greater,
C if they are equal, and D if there's not enough information to decide.

	First Item	Second Item	Response
1.	the largest prime factor of 36	the largest prime factor of 72	C
2.	the average of 3 bowling scores	the average of 6 bowling scores	
3.	the average of the first 10 odd numbers	the average of the first 10 even numbers	
4.	the greatest common factor of 16 and 25	the greatest common factor of 42 and 44	
5.	the least common multiple of 3, 4, and 8	the least common multiple of 3, 4, and 16	
6.	the product of 2 even numbers	the product of an odd and an even number	
7.	the number of perfect squares between 10 and 20	the number of perfect squares less than 10	
8.	the number of prime factors of 17^2	the number of prime factors of 19^2	

COMPLETING THE CONNECTION

Select any problem on this page and explain your thinking
in arriving at the response you selected.

MATH CONNECTIONS

Geometry and Measurement

In each row, write A if the first item is greater, B if the second item is greater,
C if they are equal, and D if there's not enough information to decide.

	First Item	Second Item	Response
1.	the complement of 89°	the supplement of 179°	C
2.	the number of centimeters in 1 meter	the number of pennies in $10	
3.	the complement of an acute angle	the supplement of an obtuse angle	
4.	the number of quarts in $5\frac{1}{2}$ gallons	21	
5.	the number of feet in 1 yard	the number of square feet in 1 square yard	
6.	the perimeter of a square with a side of 10 inches	the perimeter of an equilateral triangle with a side of 13.3 inches	
7.	the perimeter of a rectangle with a length of 5 inches	the perimeter of an equilateral triangle with a side of 5 inches	
8.	the radius of a circle with a circumference of 10π	the diameter of a circle with a circumference of 5π	

COMPLETING THE CONNECTION
Select any problem on this page and explain your thinking
in arriving at the response you selected.

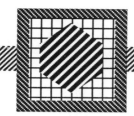

Geometry Visual

In each row, write A if the first item is greater, B if the second item is greater,
C if they are equal, and D if there's not enough information to decide.

	Illustration	First Item	Second Item	Response
1.		measure of $\angle x$	measure of $\angle y$	C
2.		measure of $\angle x$	measure of $\angle y$	
3.		0	measure of $\angle x$ minus the measure of $\angle y$	
4.		t	7	
5.		CD	AB	
6.		area of parallelogram	50	

COMPLETING THE CONNECTION

Select any problem on this page and explain your thinking
in arriving at the response you selected.

MATH CONNECTIONS

Pre-Algebra

In each row, write A if the first item is greater, B if the second item is greater,
C if they are equal, and D if there's not enough information to decide.

	First Item	Second Item	Response
1.	10^5	$10 + 10 + 10 + 10 + 10$	A
2.	$|5 + -4|$	$|5| + |-4|$	
3.	$64(-79)$	$65(-79)$	
4.	the sum of any 7 negative integers	the product of any 7 negative integers	
5.	$4a$	$5b$	
6.	$(-7)^2$	-7^2	
7.	$4a$	$a + a + a + a$	
8.	$\sqrt{50}$	$\sqrt{25} + \sqrt{25}$	

COMPLETING THE CONNECTION

Select any problem on this page and explain your thinking
in arriving at the response you selected.

Answer Section

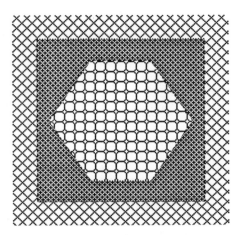

Answer Section

Section 1: Versus

Page 5 (Positive vs. Negative):
2. negative **3.** positive **4.** negative **5.** neither **6.** positive **7.** positive **8.** can't be determined **9.** positive **10.** negative

Page 6 (Greater Than vs. Less Than):
2. greater than **3.** neither **4.** greater than **5.** less than **6.** less than **7.** less than **8.** can't be determined **9.** Answers will vary. **10.** Answers will vary.

Page 7 (Factor vs. Multiple):
2. multiple **3.** factor **4.** neither **5.** multiple **6.** multiple **7.** can't be determined **8.** can't be determined **9.** Answers will vary. **10.** Answers will vary.

Page 8 (Prime vs. Composite):
2. composite **3.** composite **4.** neither **5.** composite **6.** composite **7.** composite **8.** can't be determined **9.** composite **10.** prime

Page 9 (Complement vs. Supplement):
2. supplementary **3.** neither **4.** neither **5.** supplementary **6.** complementary **7.** 28° **8.** 80° **9.** $90° - k°$ **10.** $180° - r°$

Page 10 (Square vs. Square Root):
2. square **3.** neither **4.** square root **5.** neither **6.** neither **7.** square root **8.** can't be determined **9.** 12 **10.** 0.04

Page 11 (Parallel vs. Perpendicular):
2. neither **3.** perpendicular **4.** parallel **5.** perpendicular **6.** perpendicular **7.** can't be determined **8.** $y = 6x + c$, $c \neq -3$ **9.** $y = 4x + c$, $c \neq 0$ **10.** Answers will vary (but cannot be $y = x + c$ or $y = -x + c$).

Section 2: Which One Doesn't Belong?

(Suggested answers and rationales)
Page 15 (Fractions and Decimals):
2. D; not equivalent to 3/4 **3.** B; doesn't add to 1 **4.** B; can't be reduced **5.** A; not smaller than 2 **6.** C; not a decimal for eighths **7.** A; not equivalent to 4/5 **8.** C; not equivalent to 1/8

Page 16 (Percents):
2. D; does not equal 8 **3.** D; not equivalent to 1/100 **4.** B; not equivalent to 3 1/4 **5.** C; does not equal 9 **6.** A; does not equal $8 in simple interest **7.** C; is not an increase of 50% **8.** D; is not a decrease of 10%

Page 17 (Number Theory):
2. B; not prime **3.** A; not a perfect square **4.** D; not divisible by 9 **5.** B; not divisible by 4 **6.** A; not a power of 2 **7.** D; not a perfect cube **8.** C; not in scientific notation

Page 18 (Measurement):
2. D; not a unit of mass **3.** C; not a unit of English measure **4.** D; not a metric prefix **5.** D; does not equal 10 years **6.** B; not a typical marking on a ruler **7.** A; does not equal 72 **8.** B; does not equal 1 square yard

Page 19 (Geometry):
2. D; not complementary **3.** A; not supplementary **4.** C; does not sum to 180° **5.** D; not a side classification for triangles **6.** C; not an angle classification for triangles **7.** A; not a quadrilateral **8.** B; not a Pythagorean triple

Page 20 (Geometry Visual):
2. D; not equilateral **3.** B; not convex **4.** C; not congruent **5.** D; not a condition for parallel lines

Page 21 (Pre-Algebra):
2. A; incorrect use of distributive property **3.** C; not a similar term **4.** D; does not equal 49 **5.** A; not degree 3 **6.** C; doesn't simplify to a multiple of $\sqrt{2}$ **7.** D; not a difference of 2 squares **8.** D; slope not equal to 2

Section 3: How Do You Know That?

(Suggested answers)
Page 25 (Fractions):
2. For unit fractions the smaller the denominator the greater the fraction. **3.** The 5 has to multiply both the 5 and the 1/4. **4.** A non-0 number divided by itself equals 1. **5.** 8 divided by 1/2 asks how many halves are in 8, and there are more than 8 halves in 8. **6.** 1/2 plus 2/3 is greater than 1. **7.** In the multiplication the factors will divide out, resulting in an answer of 1. **8.** Adding a positive fraction to 1/2 has to result in an answer greater than 1/2, which 2/5 is not.

Page 26 (Decimals):
2. 3.12 is between 3 and 4; therefore, the product of 3.12 x 16 must be between 48 and 64. **3.** 2 times 1000 is 2000; therefore, a number slightly more than 2 multiplied by 1000 has to be greater than 2000. **4.** Because 0.7 is greater than 0.5, the sum of 0.7 and 0.5 has to be greater than 1. **5.** There are more than 20 halves in 20. **6.** 60 is 10 times 6, and 4.2 is 1/10 of 42, and 10 times 1/10 equals 1. **7.** 3/10 does not equal 1/3. **8.** For scientific notation the number multiplying the power of 10 must be expressed as a decimal between 1 and 10.

Page 27 (Percents):
2. 0.16 times 45 equals 0.45 times 16. **3.** The total needs to be $100 for 5% to equal $5.00. **4.** 100% is all of 20; 110% would be 20 plus 10% more. **5.** 10% of 100 is 10, and 11% of 100 is 11. **6.** An increase of 100% means the number plus itself. **7.** Although the percent is doubled, the base is less than 1/2 of $420. **8.** 150% means all plus 1/2 of the total.

Page 28 (Number Theory):
2. The sum of the digits is not divisible by **3.** 3. The least common multiple must be as large as or larger than the largest number; therefore, it must be greater than 8. **4.** The sum of the numbers is equal to the number of numbers times the average of the numbers. **5.** The sum of the digits is not divisible by 9. **6.** The square root is not an integer. **7.** 12 is a factor of 36. **8.** Factors occur in pairs. If the total number of factors is an odd number, it must be that a number multiplies itself.

Page 29 (Geometry and Measurement):
2. Because there are 12 inches in 1 foot, there must be 144 square inches in 1 square foot. **3.** The ratio must be done in the same units. 5 yards equals 15 feet gives a ratio fo 1:3. **4.** Because 2 pints equal 1 quart, the cost should not be greater. **5.** Area equals side squared; if the side is doubled, the area would be 4 times the side squared. **6.** An obtuse angle is less than 180°; 1/2 of an angle less than 180° gives an angle less than 90°, or an acute angle. **7.** The sum of the 2 smaller sides of a triangle must be greater than the larger side. **8.** In a triangle any 2 sides intersect, and parallel lines do not intersect.

Page 30 (Pre-Algebra):
2. 2^{10} equals $(2^2)^5$ equals 4^5. **3.** 24 does not equal 4(9) plus 12. **4.** An odd number of negative numbers produces a negative product. **5.** 9^2 does not equal 25 plus 16. **6.** For -5^2 the order of operations indicates that you square and then use the negative to give a result of –25. **7.** $\sqrt{39}$ falls between $\sqrt{36}$ and $\sqrt{49}$. **8.** a^2 equals a times a, and $2a$ equals a plus a.

Section 4: Write a Question Pictured

(Suggested answers)
Page 33 (Geometry):
2. What is the complement of 20°? **3.** What is the supplement of 40°? **4.** If the vertex angle of an isosceles triangle measures 40°, what is the measure of 1 of the base angles? **5.** If 2 interior angles of a triangle measure 65° and 30°, what is the measure of the exterior angle at the third vertex?

Page 34 (Geometry):
2. If an obtuse angle of a parallelogram measures 130°, what is the measure of an acute angle of the parallelogram? **3.** If 1 interior angle formed by a pair of parallel lines cut by a transversal

measures 70°, what is the measure of its alternate interior angle? **4.** If an angle is bisected and 1/2 of it measures 35°, what is the measure of the entire angle? **5.** If 3 central angles of a circle sum to a semicircle and 2 of the angles measure 50° and 45°, what is the measure of the third angle?

Page 35 (Triangles):

2. If 1 side of an equiangular triangle measures 7 units, what is the measure of the other 2 sides? **3.** If a median is drawn to the base of a triangle that measures 10 units, what is the measure of 1 segment formed by the median and the base? **4.** If a right triangle has a leg of 5 units and an area of 30 square units, what is the measure of the hypotenuse? **5.** If 2 triangles are similar and the sides of the smaller triangle measure 3, 4, and 5 units, what is the measure of the longest side of the large triangle, given that the other 2 sides measure 9 and 12 units?

Page 36 (Quadrilaterals):

2. If the perimeter of a square is 24 units, what does 1 side measure? **3.** If 1 side of a parallelogram measures 5 units, what does the opposite side measure? **4.** If a 4-by-9-unit rectangle has an area equal to that of a square, what is the measure of the side of the square? **5.** If a rectangle has a base of 12 units and a diagonal of 13 units, what is its height?

Page 37 (Circles):

2. If a circle has a diameter of 24 units, what is the measure of the radius? **3.** If a circle contains 8 central angles of equal measure, what is the measure of 1 angle? **4.** If 2 concentric circles have radii of 3 and 7 units, respectively, how far apart are the 2 circles? **5.** If a central angle of a circle with a radius of 10 units measures 90°, what is the length of the arc formed by the central angle?

Page 38 (Coordinates):

2. If the endpoints of a line segment are (2, 6) and (2, –8), what is the length of the segment? **3.** If a rectangle has vertices at (4, 10), (4, 4), and (12, 4), what are the coordinates of the fourth vertex? **4.** If a horizontal line segment has an endpoint at (–2, 2) and measures 20 units, what is the *x* value of the other endpoint? **5.** If a line segment has an endpoint of (1, 5) and a midpoint of (5, 5), what are the coordinates of the other endpoint?

Page 39 (Miscellaneous):

2. If 4 of the 5 numbers whose average is 70 are 50, 60, 70, 80, what is the fifth number? **3.** If 5 more than 2 times a number is 17, what is the number? **4.** If the temperature was –10° and rises 40°, what is the resulting temperature? **5.** If A and B have a ratio of 1:3 and set A contains 4 items, how many items does set B contain?

Section 5: Help Me Pose a Problem

(Suggested answers)
Page 43 (Ratios, Proportions, and Percents):

2. the price of the television **3.** the rate of discount **4.** the total number of trees in the orchard **5.** the approximate number of words in the term paper **6.** the number of free throws Nicole made

Page 44 (Number Theory):

2. the sum of the consecutive odd numbers **3.** other characteristics of the number, for example, that it's also a multiple of 25 **4.** other characteristics of the number, for example, that it is a perfect cube larger than 1 **5.** the lengths of the 3 strands **6.** the size of a bunch of roses

Page 45 (Pre-Algebra):

2. the temperatures for the 2 remaining days **3.** give 1 integer **4.** the *y*-coordinate **5.** the coordinates of the other endpoint **6.** the coordinates of the second point

Page 46 (Geometry):

2. the measure of the larger angle (or information about the relationship of the 2 angles) **3.** the measure of the third angle (or information about the relationship of the 3 angles) **4.** the measure of 1 of the latter 2 angles (or information about the relationship of the latter 2 angles) **5.** the measure of the other leg **6.** the measure of the shortest side of the second triangle (or the measure of the middle side)

Page 47 (Area, Perimeter, and Volume):
2. the height of the triangle **3.** the width of the rectangle **4.** the length and the width of the rectangular solid **5.** the width of the floor **6.** the radius of the larger circle

Page 48 (Miscellaneous):
2. the amount of money Hilke gave to the clerk **3.** the number of pencils in a package **4.** the number of balls in a box **5.** the total cost of the house and the lot **6.** the number of nickels Lauren has

Section 6: Quantitative Comparison

Page 51 (Fractions):
2. B **3.** A **4.** C **5.** D **6.** B **7.** C **8.** B

Page 52 (Decimals):
2. B **3.** A **4.** B **5.** B **6.** C **7.** A **8.** C

Page 53 (Percents):
2. B **3.** A **4.** C **5.** C **6.** A **7.** A **8.** C

Page 54 (Number Theory):
2. D **3.** A **4.** B **5.** B **6.** D **7.** B **8.** C

Page 55 (Geometry and Measurement):
2. B **3.** D **4.** A **5.** B **6.** A **7.** D **8.** C

Page 56 (Geometry Visual):
2. A **3.** C **4.** B **5.** A **6.** B

Page 57 (Pre-Algebra):
2. B **3.** A **4.** D **5.** D **6.** A **7.** C **8.** B